FLAMINGO
Coloring Book for Adult

THIS BOOK BELONGS TO

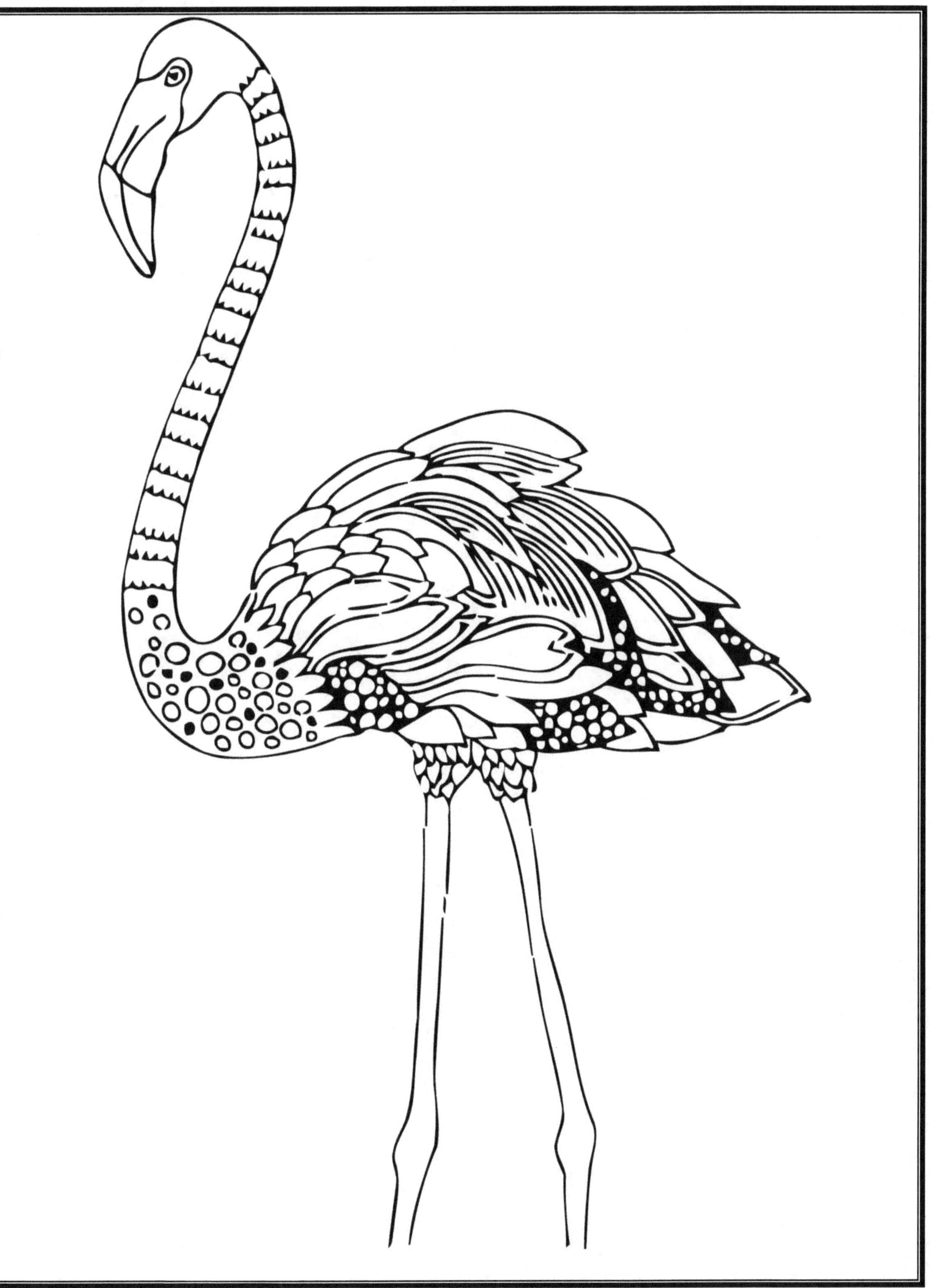

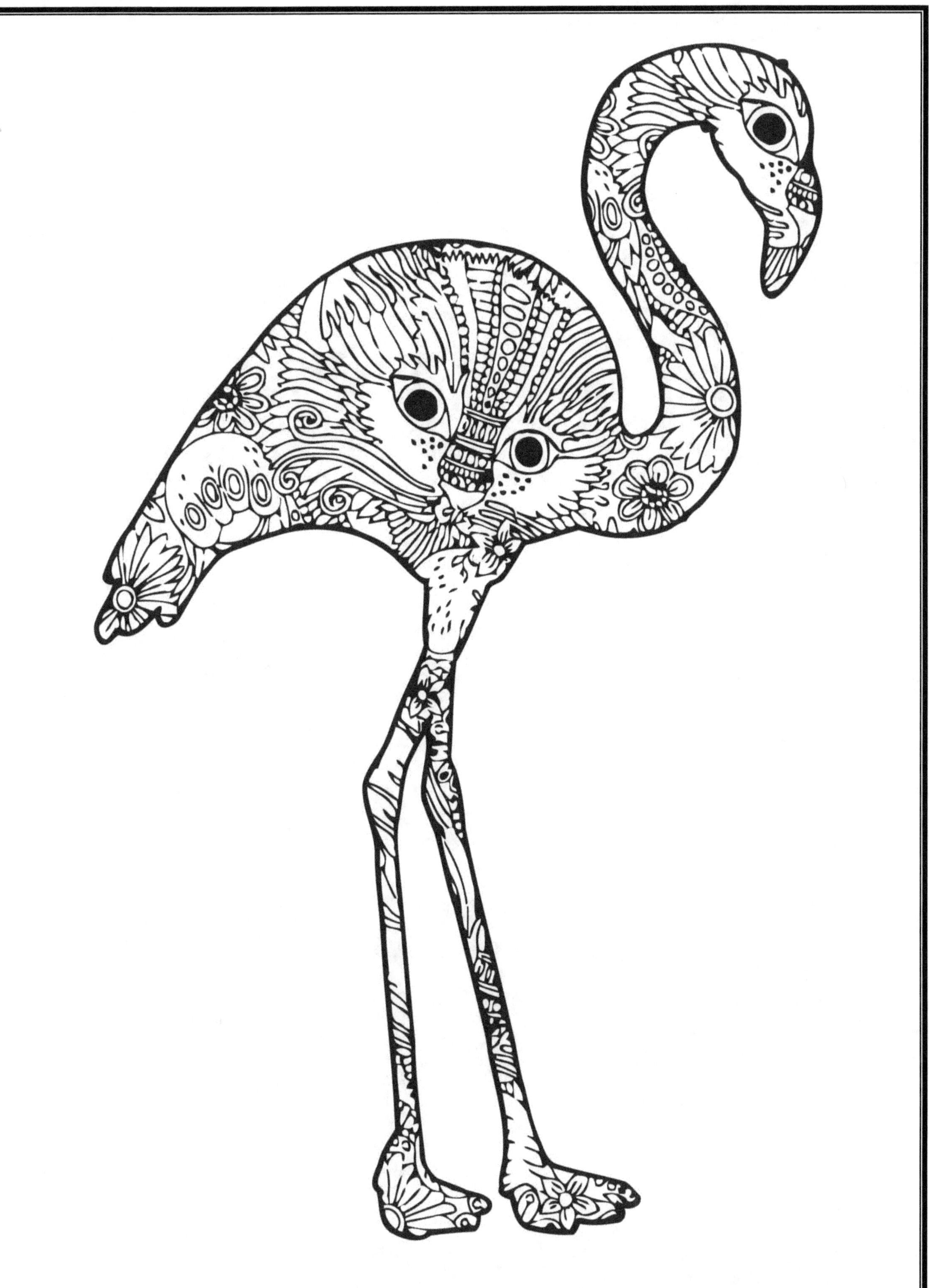

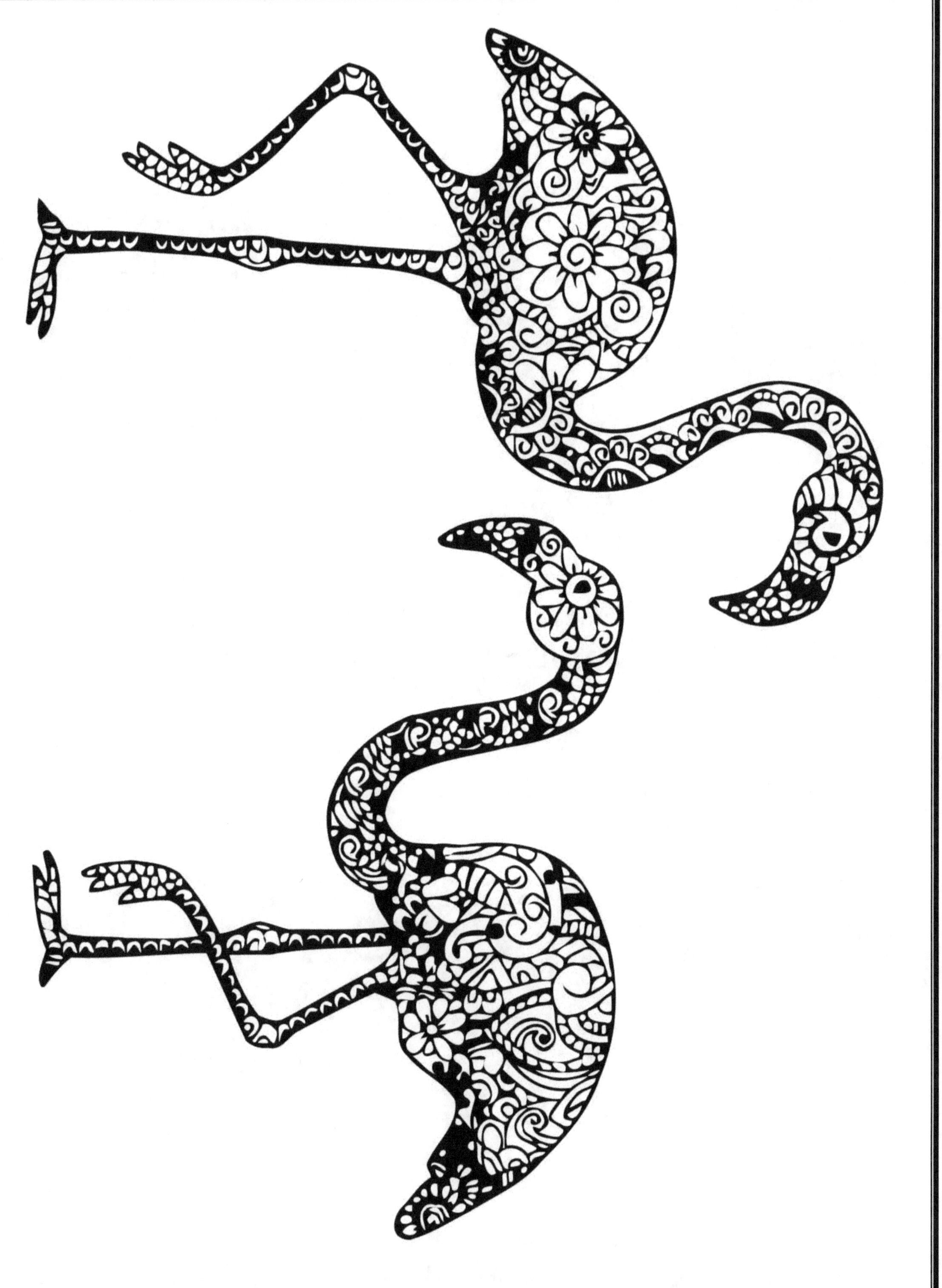

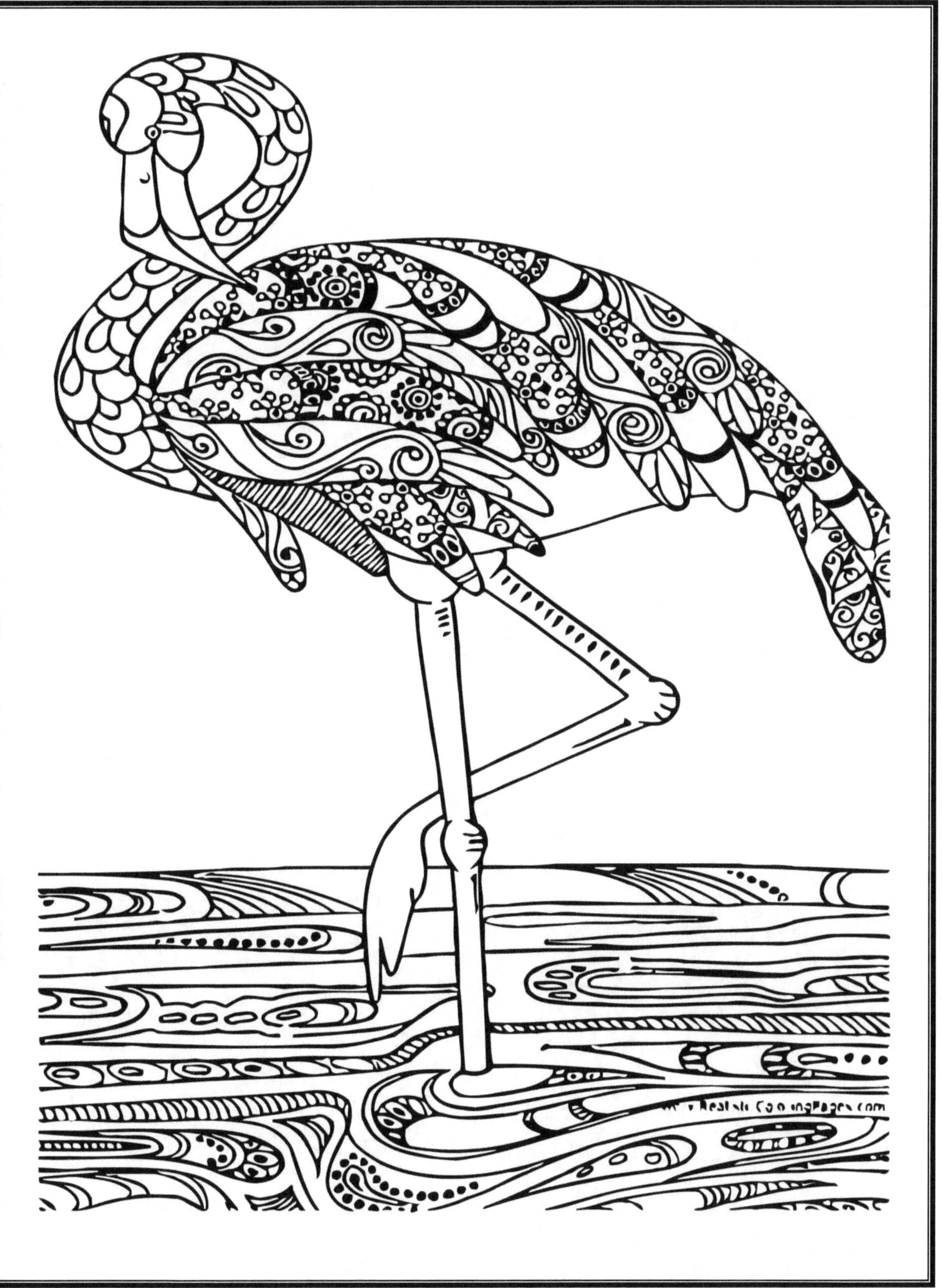
MyFreeColoringPages.com

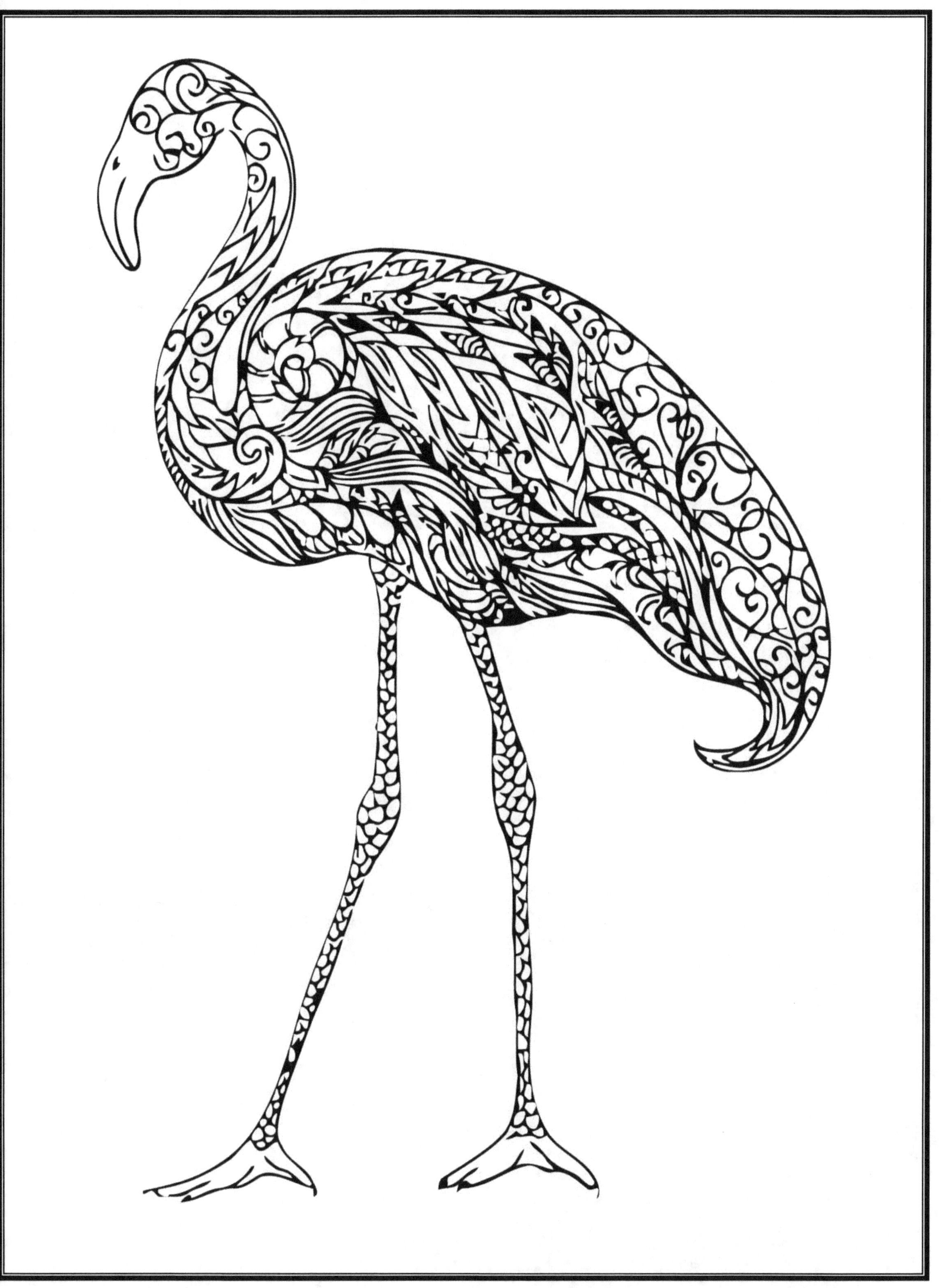

Think You
WWW.AMAZON.COM/AUTHOR/MASABPRESSHOUSE

www.ingramcontent.com/pod-product-compliance
Lightning Source LLC
Chambersburg PA
CBHW081442250726
48662CB00009B/2904

9 781677 138340